PLANT-BA
FOR BEGINNERS

MW01194655

30 SIMPLE AND TASTY RECIPES FOR EXCITING MEALS AND HEALTHY WEIGHT LOSS

J.S. WEST

[FREE eBook LIMITED offer]

As a "Thank You" note to your interest in my recipe books, I'd like to offer my latest eBook for free up to 1000 amazon kindle downloads. There aren't many left so grab your free copy now!

Click image to download

[JOIN FOR FREE]

TABLE OF CONTENTS

Introduction

I want to thank you and congratulate you for downloading the book, *"Plant-Based Whole Foods For Beginners: 30 Simple and Tasty Recipes for Exciting Meals and Healthy Weight Loss"*.

This book contains proven steps and strategies on how to get started on a plant-based whole foods diet.

Eating on a plant-based whole foods diet is a great way to lose weight, avoid food allergens, and feel great about yourself and your body! This book will provide you with thirty amazing recipes that are so delicious you won't even realize you're excluding meat, dairy, and eggs from your diet. Keep your meals exciting by following the recipes and sample meal plan outlined in this book!

Thanks again for downloading this book, I hope you enjoy it!

Chapter 1 - Plant-Based Whole Foods vs. Vegan

When it comes to keeping your body and mind both in great shape, the most important factor is to be sure you're consuming healthy, fresh foods. Never underestimate the power of eating foods that are ultra good for you! And of course, the healthiest possible food groups are fruits, vegetables, and some grains. After all, your mother knew what she was talking about when she told you to eat all your vegetables!

To ensure optimal health and fitness, consider trying a plant-based whole foods lifestyle. This does not necessarily mean you will be a vegan, although it's certainly very easy for you to take that step, as well. A plant-based whole foods lifestyle consists of eating absolutely no meat, dairy, or eggs, and also avoiding processed foods. On this diet, you will be enjoying fresh vegetables, fruit, beans, potatoes, and whole grains.

A vegan lifestyle is of course very similar, but carries over into other aspects of daily life aside from just food. Vegans also avoid using animal products in any way; they do not wear leather shoes or use fish oil based cosmetics, for example. You may choose to go this route after you begin your whole foods plant diet, but you do not have to. However, if you do make that decision, this diet is a great place to begin!

Personal ethics and weight loss are both great reasons to give a plant-based diet a try. If you feel like eating animal products is wrong, then this is a great diet for you! And if you are trying to lose weight, nothing will make those pounds melt away faster than consuming plenty of healthy vegetables. However, there are many other reasons why this type of lifestyle may be perfect for you. If you have food allergies or sensitivities, you will absolutely benefit from a plant-based lifestyle! Your digestive system and immune system both will thank you for giving this diet a try.

Please note, however, that plant-based eating is not recommended for those with gluten sensitivity or celiac disease. Many plant-based diets include whole grains, which by nature contain gluten.

If you feel like you may be interested in giving this lifestyle a try, just read on to discover thirty incredible recipes to get you started!

FRUITY QUINOA

For a simple and quick breakfast, whip up this tasty fresh fruit quinoa bowl! Make it ahead of time and store it in plastic containers or glass mason jars on the refrigerator for simple reheating and eating.

1 cup cooked quinoa

1 cup diced fresh fruit or berries

1/2 cup walnuts

Agave syrup to taste

Almond milk to taste

2 tsp cinnamon

1. Cook quinoa according to package directions.
2. Add almond milk and stir on low heat until quinoa reaches desired thickness.
3. Top with berries, walnuts, agave, and cinnamon.
4. Serve.

BREAKFAST SKILLET

This yummy breakfast skillet is easy to prepare and even easier to devour happily! Similar to scrambles but without eggs, this recipe is great in a bowl on its own or served with warm whole wheat or corn tortillas.

1 onion

1 carrot

1 green bell pepper

1 cup frozen diced hash brown potatoes

1/2 cup canned beans of you choice

1 jalapeño pepper

3 stalks asparagus

2 handfuls spinach leaves

1. Chop onion and asparagus.
2. Slice carrot, jalapeño pepper, and bell pepper.
3. Drain and rinse beans.
4. In a large skillet over medium-high heat on the stove, cook diced hash brown potatoes, stirring frequently to keep from burning.   Cook until browned.
5. Add onion and carrot to skillet and cook for 5 minutes.
6. Add bell pepper and cook for 2 minutes.
7. Add beans and jalapeño pepper and cook for 2 minutes.
8. Add spinach and asparagus, but do not stir.
9. Cover and steam for 5 minutes.
10. Serve.

MORNING SOFT TACOS

These yummy breakfast tacos are packed with delicious flavor and lots of protein to get your day off to the right start!

1 onion

1 green bell pepper

1 jalapeño pepper

1 cup white button mushrooms

1 cup cauliflower florets

1 large baking potato

1 cup canned beans of your choice

1/2 cup cooked quinoa

Corn or whole wheat tortillas

Black pepper

Minced garlic

1. Prepare quinoa according to package directions.
2. Dice onion, green bell pepper, jalapeño pepper, and mushrooms.
3. If starting from a whole head of cauliflower, chop florets from stalks.
4. Chop potato.
5. Drain and rinse beans.
6. Place onions, peppers, and mushrooms in a large skillet over medium heat on the stove. Stir and cook for 7 minutes.
7. Add potato, quinoa, and beans. Stir and cook for 5 minutes.
8. Add black pepper and minced garlic. Stir and cook for 2 minutes.
9. Serve in tortillas.

CHOCO-CHERRY OATMEAL

When you're battling an intense chocolate craving, start your day off with this delicious and ultra-sweet oatmeal bowl. As an added bonus, kids love it!

1/2 cup dry rolled oats

3/4 cup water

1/4 cup frozen cherries

1 tbsp vegan chocolate chips

1/2 tbsp pure maple syrup

1 tsp chia seeds

1. Combine dry rolled oats with water and cook according to oat packaging directions.
2. Chop frozen cherries; remove pits if not already pitted.
3. Mix cherries and chocolate chips into oatmeal while still warm.
4. Stir in maple syrup and top with chia seeds.
5. Serve.

TEX-MEX BREAKFAST BURRITOS

This easy skillet meal is great for adults and kids alike! The hearty potatoes give you plenty of energy for your morning at work or at school.

10 potatoes

1 onion

4 tbsp minced garlic

2 jalapeño peppers

Black pepper to taste

1/2 cup water

Corn or whole grain tortillas

1. Peel and dice potatoes into bite-sized pieces.
2. Dice onion and jalapeño peppers.
3. In a large skillet (or soup pot) on the stove, stir together potatoes, onion, garlic, and water.
4. Turn heat to medium and cover.
5. Cook for 30 minutes, stirring every 3 to 5 minutes to keep from sticking.
6. Place mixture in tortillas.
7. Top with jalapeño peppers and black pepper to taste.
8. Serve.

RICE PORRIDGE

This delectable and heartwarming breakfast is a traditional homey favorite that won't break the bank!

2 cups uncooked brown rice

4 cups water

2 cups almond milk

1 tbsp cinnamon

1 apple

1/4 cup raisins

1/4 cup pure maple syrup

1. Dice apple (leave peel on).
2. In a large sauce pan over medium heat, stir together rice, water, and cinnamon.
3. Cook for 30 minutes.
4. Add 1 cup almond milk, diced apples, and raisins.
5. Stir and cook for an additional 15 minutes.
6. Let cool.
7. Stir in 1 cup almond milk.
8. Serve.

MUFFINS

You don't need eggs to make excellent muffins! Just make this recipe and you can freeze or refrigerate and reheat these muffins for up to 2 weeks for easy grab-and-go breakfasts.

1 cup brown rice flour

1/2 cup sorghum flour

1/2 cup tapioca flour

1 tsp xanthan gum

1/4 cup yeast

1 tsp onion powder

1 tsp garlic powder

1/2 tsp black pepper

1 large baking potato

1 onion

1 green bell pepper

1 cup mushrooms

1 jalapeño pepper

1-3/4 cup almond milk

1. Dice baking potato, onion, bell pepper, mushrooms, and jalapeño pepper.
2. Preheat oven to 350 degrees Fahrenheit.
3. Combine rice flour, sorghum flour, tapioca flour, xanthan gum, yeast, onion powder, garlic powder, and black pepper in a large bowl and stir to mix thoroughly.
4. Add potato, onion, green bell pepper, mushrooms, and jalapeño pepper, and stir to mix thoroughly.
5. Pour in almond milk and stir to combine well.
6. Fill a muffin tin with batter.
7. Bake for 25 minutes.
8. Cool and serve.

EASY PEACH OATMEAL

Warm yourself and your family from the inside out with this easy oatmeal recipe!

4 cups dry rolled oats

2 peaches

1/4 cup pure maple syrup

2 tbsp cinnamon

2 tsp chia seeds

1. Cook oats according to packaging directions.
2. Peel and slice peaches.
3. In a large skillet on the stove over medium heat, cover peaches just barely with water and cook for 5 minutes or until soft.
4. Place half of the cooked peaches into a blender.
5. Blend on high until smooth.
6. Stir pureed peaches into oatmeal until thoroughly combined.
7. Serve topped with peach chunks, maple syrup, cinnamon, and chia seeds.

FRESH BREAKFAST PARFAIT

These are great breakfasts as well as delicious brunch desserts or appetizers for a get-together!   Mix up the fruit and nuts/seeds for plenty of delicious options!

2 cups vegan yogurt (made from almond or soy)

2 cups strawberries

1 cup granola

1 cup sunflower seeds

1. Slice strawberries in half.
2. Layer granola in a trifle dish.
3. Top with yogurt.
4. Add a layer of sunflower seeds.
5. Top with strawberries.

6. Repeat layering pattern.

7. Chill and serve.

CHIA SEED PUDDING

Similar to a porridge, this recipe utilizes the many health benefits and yummy taste and texture of chia seeds to make a unique breakfast cereal!

4 tbsp raw chia seeds

8oz almond milk

1/4 cup maple syrup

2 apples

1. Pour chia seeds into a glass mason jar.

2. Add almond milk.

3. Screw lid tightly onto mason jar and shake well.

4. Let sit 15 minutes.

5. Shake well again.

6. Chill overnight in the refrigerator.

7. Serve warm or cold, topped with maple syrup and diced apples.

POTATO SOUP

No need to be cold on a chilly winter's day when you have this tasty soup in your recipe repertoire! You can also make it well ahead of time and freeze it for easy access at a later date.

6 potatoes

4 cups water

2 carrots

1 onion

1/2 tsp garlic powder

1/8 cup yeast

1. Wash potatoes, leave skin on, and dice into bite sized pieces.
2. Slice carrots and dice onions.
3. Put potatoes, carrots, and onions into the bottom of a slow cooker and top with water.
4. Cover and cook on low for 6 hours or on high for 3 hours.
5. Stir in garlic powder and yeast when cooked.
6. Mash soup with a potato masher or immersion blender.
7. Serve.

SQUASH QUINOA SALAD

This light and luscious lunch is just as beautiful to look at as it is delicious to gobble up!

3 cups spinach leaves

1 cup cooked quinoa

1 butternut squash

1 tsp ginger

2 tbsp dried cranberries

1 onion

1. Prepare quinoa according to packaging directions.
2. Chop butternut squash and steam in 2 tbsp water in a covered skillet over medium-high heat for 10 minutes.
3. Dice steamed butternut squash.
4. Slice onions into rings and cook in same skillet until crispy.
5. In a large bowl, combine cooked quinoa, steamed butternut squash, and dried cranberries.
6. Add ginger and stir to combine thoroughly.
7. Top spinach with quinoa mixture.
8. Top salad with cooked onions.
9. Toss and serve.

TOMATO SOUP

One of the most popular varieties of soup worldwide, tomato soup is very easy to transfer to a plant-based recipe!

9 beefsteak tomatoes

1 onion

3 stalks celery

4 tbsp minced garlic

3 carrots

2 cups water

1. Wash all vegetables and place in a slow cooker, whole if possible (cut all but tomatoes if needed to fit).
2. Add water.
3. Cover and cook on low for 10 hours.
4. Blend with an immersion blender.
5. Serve.

TACO SALAD

Enjoy all the flavors of fresh taco salad with none of the meat and grease with this yummy lunchtime salad recipe! Serve with a side of Tomato Soup for a really delicious meal!

4 cups romaine lettuce

1 can black beans

1 cup cooked quinoa

2 cups frozen corn

1 cup pico de gallo or jarred salsa

1 avocado

1 lime

Corn tortilla chips

1. Thaw frozen corn (optionally, steam in microwave for a few minutes).
2. Rinse and drain black beans.

3. Prepare quinoa according to packaging directions.

4. Peel and slice avocado.

5. Juice lime.

6. In a large bowl, place lettuce, drained beans, cooked quinoa, corn, pico or salsa, and avocado.

7. Cover with lime juice.

8. Toss to combine thoroughly.

9. Serve with corn tortilla chips on the side or broken up as a topping.

MINESTRONE

Minestrone is a delectable and very simple soup that is both hearty and healthy! It'll fill you up and give you a boost of much-needed energy during a busy day.

1 onion

1 stalk celery

2 carrots

6 cups water

6 tbsp vegetable bouillon

2 tomatoes

1 cup canned green beans

1 cup canned white beans

1 cup canned red beans

1 tsp dried oregano

1 tsp garlic powder

2 cups spinach

2 cup whole grain spiral noodles

1. Dice onion and tomatoes.

2. Thinly slice celery and carrots.

3. Drain and rinse all canned beans.

4. Place onions, celery, and carrots in a large pot on the stove and cook over medium-high heat for 7 minutes.

5. Add water, vegetable bouillon, diced tomatoes, drained beans, and green beans. Stir to combine thoroughly.

6. Add dried oregano and garlic powder and stir to combine thoroughly.

7. Cover and simmer for 15 minutes.

8. Add spinach and noodles.

9. Cover and simmer for 15 minutes more.

10. Serve.

Chapter 4 - 10 Dinner Recipes

Shepherd's Pie

This recipe allows for easy modification of this traditionally meat-based classic comfort food.

4 potatoes

1/4 cup yeast

1-1/2 cup almond milk

2 cups lentils

2 stalks celery

2 carrots

1 onion

1/2 cup white button mushrooms

1/4 cup frozen green beans

1/4 cup frozen green peas

2 tbsp brown rice flour

Onion powder to taste

Garlic powder to taste

Black pepper to taste

1. Peel potatoes and dice into chunks.
2. Cook lentils to desired doneness.
3. Dice carrots, celery, onions, and mushrooms.
4. In a large pot on the stove over high heat, boil potatoes covered until soft.
5. Drain and mash potatoes.

6. Add 1/4 cup almond milk and yeast to potatoes and whip together.
7. Pack cooked lentils into the bottom of a pie pan to make the base layer.
8. In a large skillet on the stove over medium-high heat, cook carrots, celery, and onion until soft.
9. Add mushrooms, green beans, and green peas, and cook for an additional 5 minutes longer.
10. Add brown rice flour and stir.
11. Add almond milk and stir to thicken.
12. Season with garlic powder, onion powder, and black pepper and stir until gravy-like consistency is achieved.
13. Pour sauce over lentils layer.
14. Top with potatoes.
15. Broil for 10 minutes.
16. Serve hot.

VEGGIE BURGER

No need to exclude a weekly burger night from your meal rotation! Just make these tasty veggie burger patties and you'll be set!

1/2 can red kidney beans

1/3 cup cooked quinoa

1 onion

1 tsp chili powder

1 tsp garlic powder

1 tsp black pepper

1 tbsp tomato sauce

Buns

1. Prepare quinoa according to packaging directions.
2. Drain and rinse beans.
3. Dice onions.
4. Preheat oven to 350 degrees Fahnreheit.
5. Mash beans well into a large bowl.
6. Combine mashed beans with cooked quinoa and onions.
7. Add chili powder, garlic powder, and black pepper, and stir to combine thoroughly.
8. Add tomato sauce and stir again.
9. Make mixture into patties and place on a cookie sheet.
10. Bake for 15 minutes, flip, and bake again for 15 minutes more.
11. Serve on buns.

MEXICAN CASSEROLE

For a spicy dinner option, mix up this ultra easy and quick Mexican Casserole and watch it disappear even quicker than you made it!

1 cup uncooked brown rice

3 cups water

8oz can tomato sauce

1 tsp onion powder

1 tsp chili powder

1 tsp garlic powder

1 can black beans

1. Drain and rinse beans.
2. Place rice into the bottom of a slow cooker.
3. Top with water, tomato sauce, onion powder, chili powder, garlic powder, and black beans.
4. Stir to combine ingredients well.
5. Cover and cook on high for 4 hours.
6. Serve hot.

BARBECUE SANDWICH

This barbecue uses spaghetti squash as its whole food plant base with astonishingly delicious results!

1 large spaghetti squash

2 tbsp water

1 bottle barbecue sauce

1 package buns

1. Slice spaghetti squash in half lengthwise and place in a shallow microwave-safe dish.
2. Remove seeds from squash.
3. Pour 1 tbsp water into each half of squash.
4. Microwave for 10 minutes or until flesh can be pierced easily with a fork.

5. Shred flesh into long noodle-like strands.

6. Pour barbecue sauce over squash noodles.

7. Mix to coat thoroughly.

8. Top buns with mixture.

9. Serve.

PAD THAI

Asian food is often vegetarian anyway, so altering it to be plant-based entirely is very simple.   This recipe proves it.

1 box brown rice Pad Thai noodles

1 bag frozen stir-fry vegetables

4 cups shredded cabbage

1/4 cup soy sauce

1/4 cup sun butter

1/4 cup water

2 tbsp Sriracha sauce

1. Boil water in a large pot over high heat on the stove.

2. Add noodles and cook for 5 minutes.

3. While boiling, cook vegetables until tender in a large skillet over medium-high heat.

4. In a small bowl, combine soy sauce and sun butter with a bit of water.

5. Drain noodles.

6. Pour noodles into vegetables.

7. Top with sauce and stir to coat well.

8.   Serve hot.

MUSHROOM FAJITAS

This unique and exciting recipe makes a delicious dinner or a fun party food!

1 large portobello mushroom

1 onion

1 green bell pepper

1 cup vegetable broth

1 tsp garlic powder

1 tsp onion powder

1 tsp chili powder

1 tsp Worcestershire sauce

1 tsp liquid smoke

1 tbsp balsamic vinegar

Corn or wheat tortillas

1.   Slice mushroom, onion, and bell pepper.
2.   Combine garlic powder, onion powder, chili powder, Worcestershire sauce, liquid smoke, balsamic vinegar, and vegetable broth.   Stir.
3.   Marinate mushrooms, onion, and green bell pepper for 30 minutes in mixture.
4.   Broil mushrooms for 5 minutes per side.
5.   Cool and serve mixture in warm tortillas.

PORTOBELLO BURGERS

If you prefer something a little heartier than the Veggie Burger recipe, make these amazing Portobello Burgers. You'll feel like you're eating meat—but you won't be!

1 tbsp Worcestershire sauce

1 tbsp liquid smoke

1 tbsp agave syrup

1/2 cup water

4 large portobello mushrooms

4 burger buns

1. Combine Worcestershire sauce, liquid smoke, agave syrup, and water in a small bowl and stir.
2. Rinse and dry mushrooms, and remove stems.
3. Marinate in mixture for 15 minutes; flip and marinate for 15 minutes more.
4. Grill for 10 minutes per side.
5. Serve on buns.

PIZZA SKILLET

This simple recipe takes almost no time to make and it's always a hit with kids!

16oz wheat noodles of any kind

1 red bell pepper

2 roma tomatoes

1 onion

4 Portabello mushrooms

1 jar pasta sauce

1. Dice bell pepper, tomatoes, onions, and mushrooms.
2. Boil water in a pot and cook noodles according to packaging directions.
3. Add bell pepper, tomatoes, onion, and mushrooms to boiled noodles and cover.
4. Boil covered for 5 minutes.
5. Drain and add pasta sauce.
6. Stir to combine thoroughly.
7. Serve hot.

PASTA BAKE

Delicious Italian flavors meld together perfectly in this yummy and simple recipe.

1 package spiral whole grain noodles

1 eggplant

3 cups kale

3 cups broccoli

1 red bell pepper

1 jar pasta sauce

Garlic powder to taste

Onion powder to taste

Vegan cheese to taste

1. In a large pot over high heat, boil 3/4 pot of water.

2. Peel and cube eggplant.

3. Dice red bell pepper.

4. Add uncooked noodles and eggplant.

5. Boil for 10 minutes.

6. Add broccoli and red bell pepper and boil for 5 minutes more.

7. Add chopped kale and boil for 2 minutes more.

8. Drain water.

9. Add pasta sauce, onion powder, garlic powder, and vegan cheese and stir to combine thoroughly.

10. Serve hot.

POT PIE

Pot Pie isn't just for chicken anymore! Make this scrumptious vegetable based pot pie to stick to your plant-based diet and enjoy every bite!

3 cups water

2 potatoes

2 carrots

2 stalks celery

1 onion

1 cup canned green beans

2 cups wheat pastry flour

1 tsp baking powder

1/2 tsp baking soda

1 cup almond milk

1/2 cup vegetable broth

1 tbsp corn starch

1. Drain green beans.
2. Peel and dice potatoes and onion.
3. Slice celery and carrots.
4. Boil water in a large pot on the stove over high heat.
5. Add potatoes, carrots, celery, and onion.
6. Cover and cook for 10 minutes.
7. Add green beans and cook uncovered for 5 more minutes.
8. Remove from heat.
9. Preheat oven to 425 degrees Fahrenheit.
10. Combine pastry flour, baking powder, and baking soda in a large bowl and mix well.
11. Pour in 3/4 cup almond milk and stir well to combine thoroughly.
12. Spread half of the wet dough into a pie plate to cover the bottom and sides.
13. In a small bowl, combine corn starch with vegetable broth and 1/4 cup almond milk to create a sauce.
14. Top pie crust with lots of cooked vegetables.
15. Top with sauce.
16. Spread remaining wet dough onto vegetables.
17. Bake for 15 minutes
18. Cool   and   serve.

BASIC BROWNIES

Nothing beats a brownie for a basic and ultra yummy dessert. Keep kids and adults both happy with these great sweets!

1/4 cup applesauce

2/3 cup cocoa powder

1/4 cup brown rice flour

1/4 cup sorghum flour

1/4 tsp baking powder

1/2 cup turbinado sugar

1 sweet potato

1-1/2 tsp vanilla

1/4 cup almond milk

1/2 cup vegan chocolate chips

1. Pierce sweet potato with a fork a few times and cook in the microwave for 5 minutes.
2. Mash sweet potato with a potato masher into a small bowl.
3. Preheat oven to 350 degrees Fahrenheit.
4. In a large bowl, combine applesauce, cocoa powder, rice flour, sorghum flour, baking powder, turbinado sugar, mashed sweet potato, vanilla extract, and almond mix.
5. Stir to mix thoroughly together to form a batter.
6. Fold in chocolate chips.

7. Bake in a baking pan for 50 minutes.

8. Cool and serve.

CHOCO-CHIP BARS

This recipe makes an excellent alternative to cookies that still provides all the flavors of a chocolate chip cookie!

1/2 cup sun butter (sunflower seed spread)

1/2 cup sugar

1/2 cup brown rice flour

1/2 cup sorghum flour

1/2 tsp xanthan gum

1/2 tsp vanilla extract

1/4 cup almond milk

1/2 cup vegan chocolate chips

1. Preheat oven to 350 degrees Fahrenheit.

2. In a large bowl, cream together sun butter and sugar.

3. Add rice flour, sorghum flour, xanthan gum, vanilla extract, and almond milk and stir to combine thoroughly to form a dough.

4. Fold in vegan chocolate chips.

5. Bake in a baking pan for 12 minutes.

6. Cool and cut into bars.

7. Serve.

PUMPKIN CAKE

For a tasty fall treat, look no further than this autumnal recipe!

2 cups wheat pastry flour

1 tsp baking powder

1/2 tsp baking soda

1 tsp pumpkin pie spice

1 can pumpkin

1 cup pure maple syrup

1 tsp vanilla extract

1/2 cup almond milk

1. Preheat oven to 350 degrees Fahrenheit.
2. Combine flour, baking powder, baking soda, pumpkin pie spice, and pumpkin in a large bowl.
3. In a separate small bowl, combine maple syrup, vanilla extract, and almond milk, and stir until completely mixed.
4. Pour liquid ingredients into dry ingredients and mix into a batter.
5. Bake in a cake pan for 40 minutes.
6. Serve.

RHUBARB PIE

This traditional Southern style treat is perfect for a home cooked dessert the whole family will love! Take it on a picnic and wow everybody!

1 premade wheat pie crust

4 stalks rhubarb

3 cups strawberries

1-1/2 cup sugar

3/4 cup tapioca flour

1/2 tsp balsamic vinegar

1/2 cup dry rolled oats

1/2 cup unsweetened applesauce

1. Preheat oven to 400 degrees Fahrenheit.
2. Thaw pie crust if necessary.
3. Dice rhubarb and slice strawberries in half.
4. Combine rhubarb, strawberries, 1 cup sugar, 1/4 cup tapioca flour, and balsamic vinegar in a large bowl and mix thoroughly.
5. Poke holes into pie crust.
6. Pour filling into pie crust.
7. In a blender, combine rolled oats, unsweetened applesauce, 1/2 cup sugar, and 1/2 cup tapioca flour.
8. Blend on high until mixed like a batter.
9. Spoon mixture onto top of pie.
10. Cover pie with foil loosely.
11. Bake for 10 minutes.
12. Reduce oven temperature to 350 degrees Fahrenheit and bake for 40 minutes.
13. Remove foil and bake for 10 minutes.
14. Cool and serve.

SUNFLOWER COOKIES

These cookies will make you feel bright and sunny, just like the flowers the sunflower seeds came from. Don't feel guilty about enjoying a second one!

1/4 cup unsweetened applesauce

1/2 cup sun butter

1/2 cup sugar

1/2 tsp vanilla extract

1/4 cup warm water

1 tbsp chia seeds

1/4 tsp baking soda

1/4 cup brown rice flour

1/4 cup sorghum flour

1/4 cup tapioca flour

1/2 tsp xanthan gum

1. Preheat oven to 350 degrees Fahrenheit.
2. In a large bowl, cream together applesauce, sun butter, sugar, and vanilla extract.
3. In a separate smaller bowl, mix together warm water and chia seeds and let sit.
4. In a separate large bowl, combine baking soda, rice flour, sorghum flour, tapioca flour, and xanthan gum and mix well.
5. Pour liquid ingredients (including chia seeds) into dry ingredients and combine thoroughly.

6.   Roll out balls of dough and place on cookie sheet.

7.   Bake for 12 minutes.

8.   Serve.

Chapter 6 - Week-Long Meal Plan and Daily Shopping Lists

This chapter outlines a sample week-long meal plan and shopping lists broken down by each day of the week for your ease of access and convenience. Reference this list for ideas, or copy it exactly for your first week eating a plant-based whole foods diet!

When planning your weekly meals, be sure to consider the possibilities of eating leftovers! Leftovers from a night or two before make excellent lunches, and can cut down on the cost of required ingredients for the week by a lot. This meal plan is working on the assumption that you will not have very many leftovers, so it includes different lunch options throughout the week. However, feel free to tweak it as necessary to suit your needs!

Many of the recipes are repeated for breakfasts and lunches in this meal plan. This is because these recipes are able to be made ahead of time and stored in mason jars for quick access and simple reheating when you need to eat them. You can make most of the listed breakfasts and lunches ahead of time all on the same day, saving you lots of time and hassle on your busy weekdays!

Keep in mind that the ingredients needed for each day are all listed. However, if you have already made Choco-Cherry Oatmeal for the entire week, for example, you will not need to purchase the ingredients to make it again, as it makes plenty of servings to get you through a week of breakfasts. The same is true of the other repeat breakfast and lunch recipes listed here.

Be sure to go through the ingredients listed for each day and check off those which you have already purchased or which may already be in your pantry or refrigerator!

Monday

Breakfast - Choco-Cherry Oatmeal

Lunch - Tomato Soup

Dinner - Mexican Casserole

Shopping List

Dry rolled oats

Frozen cherries

Vegan chocolate chips

Pure maple syrup

Chia seeds

9 beefsteak tomatoes

1 onion

Celery

Minced garlic

3 carrots

Dry brown rice

8oz can tomato sauce

Onion powder

Chili powder

Garlic powder

1 can black beans

Tuesday

Breakfast - Chia Seed Pudding

Lunch - Taco Salad

Dinner - Barbecue Sandwich

Shopping List

Chia seeds

Almond milk

Pure maple syrup

2 apples

Romaine lettuce

1 can black beans

Quinoa

Frozen corn

Pico de gallo or jarred salsa

1 avocado

1 lime

Corn tortilla chips

1 large spaghetti squash

1 bottle barbecue sauce

Buns

Wednesday

Breakfast - Choco-Cherry Oatmeal

Lunch - Tomato Soup

Dinner - Pad Thai

Shopping List

Dry rolled oats

Frozen cherries

Vegan chocolate chips

Pure maple syrup

Chia seeds

9 beefsteak tomatoes

1 onion

Celery

Minced garlic

3 carrots

Brown rice Pad Thai noodles

Bag frozen stir-fry vegetables

Cabbage

Soy sauce

Sun butter

Sriracha sauce

Thursday

Breakfast - Chia Seed Pudding

Lunch - Taco Salad

Dinner - Mushroom Fajitas

Shopping List

Chia seeds

Almond milk

Pure maple syrup

2 apples

Romaine lettuce

1 can black beans

Quinoa

Frozen corn

Pico de gallo or jarred salsa

1 avocado

1 lime

Corn tortilla chips

Portobello mushroom

1 onion

1 green bell pepper

Vegetable broth

Garlic powder

Onion powder

Chili powder

Worcestershire sauce

Liquid smoke

Balsamic vinegar

Corn or wheat tortillas

Friday
Breakfast - Choco-Cherry Oatmeal
Lunch - Tomato Soup
Dinner - Pizza Skillet
Shopping List
Dry rolled oats
Frozen cherries
Vegan chocolate chips
Pure maple syrup
Chia seeds
9 beefsteak tomatoes
1 onion
Celery

Minced garlic

3 carrots

16oz wheat noodles

1 red bell pepper

2 roma tomatoes

4 portobello mushrooms

1 jar pasta sauce

Saturday

Breakfast - Breakfast Skillet

Lunch - Leftovers from weekly dinners

Dinner - Portobello Burgers

Shopping List

1 onion

1 carrot

1 green bell pepper

Frozen diced hash brown potatoes

Canned beans of your choice

1 jalapeño pepper

Asparagus

Spinach

Worcestershire sauce

Liquid smoke

Agave syrup

4 large portobello mushrooms

Buns

Sunday

Breakfast - Chia Seed Pudding

Lunch - Taco Salad

Dinner - Pasta Bake

Shopping List

Chia seeds

Almond milk

Pure maple syrup

2 apples

Romaine lettuce

1 can black beans

Quinoa

Frozen corn

Pico de gallo or jarred salsa

1 avocado

1 lime

Corn tortilla chips

1 package spiral whole grain noodles

1 eggplant

Kale

Broccoli

1 red bell pepper

1 jar pasta sauce

Garlic powder

Onion powder

Vegan   cheese

Conclusion

Thank you again for downloading this book!

I hope this book was able to help you to understand how easy, delicious, and healthy plant-based whole foods dieting can be.

The next step is to start chopping those veggies and get cooking!

OTHER RECOMMENDED BOOKS

<u>Forks Over Knives-The Cookbook: Over 300 Recipes for Plant-Based Eating All Through the Year (Click to on title go to Amazon link)</u>

Book Description

Forks Over Knives—the book, the film, the movement—is back again in a Cookbook. The secret is out: If you want to lose weight, lower your cholesterol, and prevent (or even reverse!) chronic conditions such as heart disease and type 2 diabetes, the right food is your best medicine. Thousands of people have cut out meat, dairy, and oils and seen amazing results. If you're among them—or you'd like to be—you need this cookbook.

Del Sroufe, the man behind some of the mouthwatering meals in the film, proves that the Forks Over Knives philosophy is not about what you can't eat, but what you can. Chef Del and his collaborators Julieanna Hever, Judy Micklewright, Isa Chandra Moskowitz, and Darshana Thacker transform wholesome fruits, vegetables, grains, and legumes into 300 recipes—classic and unexpected, globally and seasonally inspired, and for every meal of the day, all through the year:

This is A Preview Of What You'll Learn...

Breakfast: Very Berry Smoothie, Breakfast Quinoa with Apple Compote

Salads, Soups and Stews: Kale Salad with Maple-Mustard Dressing, Lotsa Vegetable Chowder, Lucky Black-Eyed Pea Stew

Pasta and Noodle Dishes: Sicilian Cauliflower Linguine, Stir-Fried Noodles with Spring Vegetables

Stir-Fried, Grilled and Hashed Vegetables: Grilled Eggplant Steaks

Baked and Stuffed Vegetables: Millet-Stuffed Chard Rolls

The Amazing Bean: White Beans and Escarole with Parsnips

Great Grains: Polenta Pizza with Tomatoes and Basil

Desserts: Apricot Fig Squares, Bursting with Berries Cobbler

OTHER BOOKS FROM J.S. WEST

Amazon
Kindle

Click Images
for Links

*go to
J.S. West
Author Page*

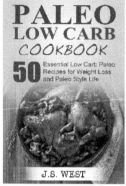

Amazon
Kindle

Click Images
for Links

go to
J.S. West
Author Page

OTHER BOOKS FROM J.S. WEST

Paleo Diet: Paleo Low Carb Slow Cooker Recipes for Beginners - Weight Loss and Paleo Style (Click to on title go to Amazon link)

Book Description

Many people in today's society are unhappy with the state of their health and wellbeing. Some want to lose weight; others have frequent stomach upset that interferes with daily life. Still others have skin problems or emotional irritability that can be easily related to eating foods that are not healthy for the body.

Early man did not have these kinds of problems. "Cavemen," as most people refer to them, ate what they could hunt, find, and pluck from the trees. They were fit and not overweight, and were generally quite healthy. The paleo diet is a recent lifestyle based on the overall food consumption of the early man, and the trend is quickly gaining popularity. It has many proven and documented health benefits, including weight loss, improved digestive systems, and increased energy levels without the use of caffeine.

This book should serve as a helpful resource for anyone looking to get started on a paleo diet. The first part of the book will explain, briefly, the definition of a paleo diet, what can and cannot be eaten when following a paleo diet, and the items most necessary to keep in stock in a paleo-friendly kitchen.

The rest of the book will be devoted to paleo recipes that can be cooked either completely or almost completely in a slow cooker. These recipes will be simple, but tasty, and will be perfect options for those who are just beginning to learn about paleo dieting. A slow cooker is a very easy and affordable option for cooking new recipes and starting a new diet, since the food can be prepared ahead of time and kept warm safely for hours.

This is A Preview Of What You'll Learn...

You will be excited and ready to try eating "like a caveman" in your own life. The health and wellness benefits will be incredible!

an understanding of the paleo diet and its benefits

what ingredients you need to set up a paleo kitchen

easy and delicious paleo slow cooker recipes

sample paleo meal plans

and much, much more!

[JOIN FOR FREE]

If you liked this book I'm sure that YOU will LIKE my other books as well.
Join my mailing list and get updates on FREE deals, new releases, bonus content and many others.
Click Here To Join for FREE

THANK YOU!!

Thank you again for downloading our book!

I hope this book was able to help you to achieve your health goals.

The next step is to apply what you've learned in this book and try out the great recipes provided.

If you enjoyed this book, please share your thoughts and leave a review on Amazon. Your feedback is important to us in order to improve the quality of the book.

CLICK HERE to LEAVE REVIEW

Good luck!

Made in the USA
Lexington, KY
30 August 2017